GHOSTS OF THE SOUTHWEST

Ghosts of the Southwest

The Phantom Gunslinger

and Other Real-Life Hauntings

TED WOOD

WALKER AND COMPANY

NEW YORK

For Beth, my talented ghost, without whom this book would have been only half as fun and twice as scary to do.

First published in the United States of America in 1997 by Walker Publishing Company, Inc.

Published simultaneously in Canada by Thomas Allen & Son Canada, Limited, Markham, Ontario

Library of Congress Cataloging-in-Publication Data
Wood, Ted.
Ghosts of the Southwest: the phantom gunslinger and other real-life hauntings/Ted Wood.
p. cm. —(Haunted America)
Includes index.
Summary: Describes homes and hotels, restaurants and towns in Arizona, New Mexico, Oklahoma, and Texas and the ghosts that haunt them.
ISBN 0-8027-8482-8 (hardcover). —ISBN 0-8027-8483-6 (reinforced)
1. Ghosts—Southwest, New—Juvenile literature. [1. Ghosts. 2. Southwest, New—Description and travel.] I. Title. II. Series.
BF1472.U6W66 1997
133.1'0979—dc20   96-38630
CIP
AC

Book design by Diane Stevenson of Snap-Haus Graphics
Maps created by Susan and Mark Carlson

Printed in Hong Kong
10 9 8 7 6 5 4 3 2 1

CONTENTS

INTRODUCTION

Sure there's a ghost here," the motel owner in Tombstone, Arizona, told me. "Drive over the San Pedro River tonight, and you might see her on the old bridge."

"A river ghost?" I asked. "Doesn't she have a house or a cemetery to haunt?"

"Not La Llorona, 'The Weeping Woman,'" he said. "She cries and searches the riverbanks for her children, whom she drowned one hundred years ago. Her soul is forever bound to the river. But be

Lucky drivers might spot the ghost of La Llorona, the Weeping Woman, roaming the San Pedro River bridge near Tombstone, looking for her drowned children.

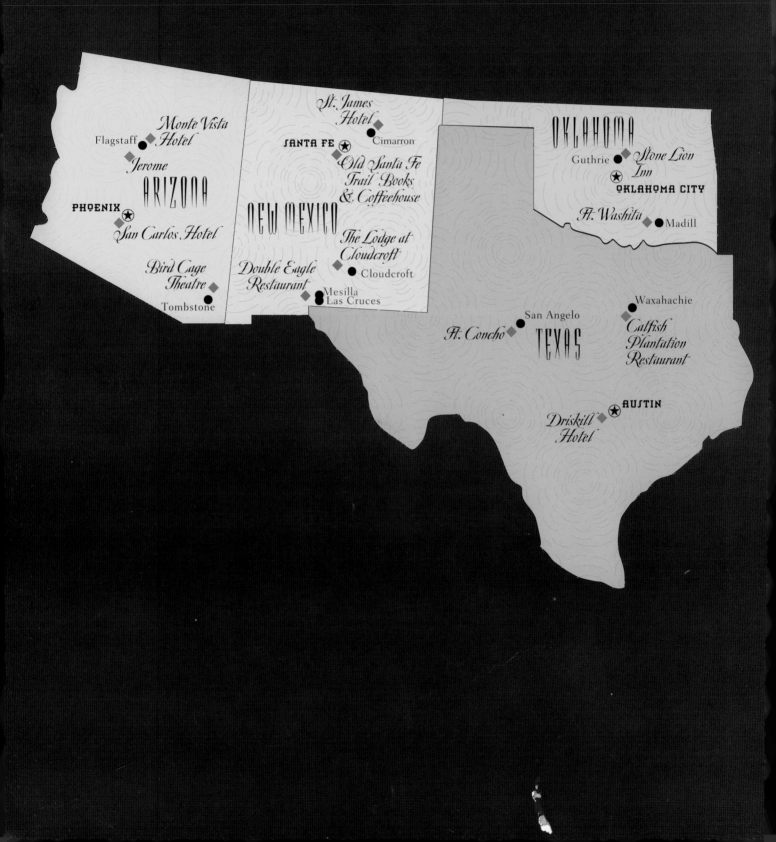

careful. If you should pass a shimmering white form floating down the road, be sure to pick her up. She won't hurt you, and when you reach the river, she'll disappear. But if you don't give her a ride, something terrible will happen to you within five miles."

Though I never saw the weeping lady in white, I learned my first lesson in ghost hunting: Ghosts can be anywhere someone died suddenly or wrongfully. Ghosts can be children, students, men and women with broken hearts, Indians, western outlaws, and even dogs! Their spirits remain in the places they died, stuck, for some reason, on Earth.

For this book, I traveled through Arizona, New Mexico, Oklahoma, and Texas looking for places haunted by these restless souls. The stories were told to me by people who work or live with their resident spooks, and I have no reason to think they were pulling my leg. Their experiences were mysteriously alike.

It seems ghosts everywhere play similar tricks. They love electricity, turning on and off lights, fans, and radios. They hide objects, spin silverware, and roll toilet paper in front of helpless, shocked bathroom users (one of their favorite tricks)!

But more often, you only sense but don't see a presence near you. A cold spot appears in a warm room, you feel invisible eyes watching, footsteps and voices fill empty halls, doors open and close. Ghosts, I am told, just want us to know they're around, especially when change comes to their homes. Most aren't mean. In fact, they're quite shy and rarely appear to more than one person. And if you're looking for them, as I was, they stay hidden—well, most of the time.

All the places described in this book are open for visits. The photographs show the actual buildings and the exact spots where the ghosts are seen. The ghosts themselves are my tricks since I couldn't get the real ones to pose. I didn't include private homes that are haunted, fearing young ghost hunters might sneak around their bushes at night, scaring the humans more than they already are. Read the book as only a book, or use it as a guide to a ghostly encounter. But remember, if you see La Llorona on the road at night, you'd better pick her up!

ARIZONA

Monte Vista Hotel, Flagstaff

HAUNTED BY

An outlaw and other phantoms

Monte Vista Hotel

Flagstaff

Jerome

ARIZONA

PHOENIX

San Carlos Hotel

Bird Cage Theatre

Tombstone

*I*n the 1920s, two gunmen robbed the bank next to the Monte Vista Hotel. They made a promise to each other: After the heist they would have

Flagstaff's ghost palace is the Monte Vista Hotel, but where the ghosts came from remains a mystery.

11

Is it a lovelorn ghost in Room 305 who moves the chair next to the window every night? No one knows for sure.

a drink in the hotel bar. But luck wasn't with the two that day; a bank guard shot one of the robbers as they fled. Even so, the wounded man insisted on keeping the promise, and the bleeding thief shared his last drink with his friend. He died in the hotel bar.

Johnny Johnson, who once owned the Monte Vista, used to hear an eerie voice that said "Hello" or "Good morning" when he opened the bar each day. He suspects the mysterious greeting came from the dead bank robber. But since he never saw the ghostly gunman, he's not sure.

The hotel has such a Wild West past—shootings, cowboys on horseback in the lobby, drunken brawls—that Johnny can't be sure who any of the ghosts are. Employees and guests have heard band music coming from the second-floor lobby. Others claim to have seen a transparent bellboy who knocks on doors and disappears. On the second floor, a woman was murdered in her room. The hotel avoids putting guests with pets there because dogs go crazy with fear and tear up the room.

The most active room is also the most mysterious. In Room 305 there's a rocking chair. No matter where in the room the cleaning staff moves the chair, the next morning it appears in the same place next to the window. Is this patient presence watching for someone on the street below, or does this ghost simply love a view? No one knows. Only the ghosts know the secrets of the Monte Vista.

Jerome, an old gold-mining town

HAUNTED BY

Ghosts of miners and maidens

If ever there was a living ghost town, Jerome is it. In fact, there may be more ghosts than people there. The mountain town sprouted overnight with the discovery of gold in the late 1890s but was abandoned just as quickly when the gold ran out. In the 1960s adventurous souls moved back to Jerome to fix up the eerie, empty buildings. But were they really empty?

Apparently not, because as soon as construction began, the buildings came alive with the dead. Eric Jurisin owns a hamburger restaurant. While he was remodeling the building, he couldn't come up with a good name for his new eatery. But then, strange things started happening. His hammers disappeared when he'd turn his back.

If you're looking for spooks of any kind in Jerome, the Spirit Room in Hotel Connor is a good place to start.

Jerome calls itself a ghost town, not because it's so empty of people but because it's so full of ghosts.

Lights turned off suddenly, doors slammed in his face, and the basement toilet flushed on its own. When he'd arrive in the morning, hot water poured from the kitchen faucet, turned on by an unseen hand.

Now, Eric didn't know anything about Jerome's spirit community, until one day a neighbor asked, "How's your haunted hamburger place going?" That's it, Eric thought, I've got the name! When he told his wife, Michelle, the name, otherworldly ears must have overheard. Shortly after, his three missing hammers reappeared. The ghosts had approved his name: The Haunted Hamburger.

Down the hill, the Inn at Jerome has a guardian ghost. Jenny Banters and her cat still watch over the hotel they once lived in. In her old haunt, the Lariat and Lace Room, Jenny keeps the cleaning staff hopping by suddenly turning on the bedside radio, rotating the ceiling fan, and moving furniture. Once when she was really annoyed she opened the dresser drawer and tossed a white bathrobe across the room. Apparently, she likes things done her way.

Though every haunted business in Jerome claims to have the best ghost, they all admit with goose bumps that the most terrifying place in town is the old, empty hospital on the hill. This forbidding building was the last stop for hundreds of injured miners, and every caretaker since the hospital closed has died a grizzly death. Jerome locals dare each other to spend the night in the haunt, but few can stomach the sounds of ghost dogs scratching at the doors and the moans echoing in the hallways. One visitor was even cut by an invisible scalpel. But the good news is that the hospital is reopening as the Grand Hotel. Now anyone can spend the night. Are you brave enough?

Soon to be a hotel, and probably a haunted one, the old hospital on the hill is the spookiest building in Jerome.

San Carlos Hotel, downtown Phoenix

HAUNTED BY
Heartbroken Leone and three little boys

On the seventh floor of the San Carlos Hotel, there's a brokenhearted ghost who still waits for her lost love. But the three old ladies who recently checked into a room on the same floor didn't know about the sad spirit. They came to Phoenix for a fun-filled night on the town. The hot trip had made them sweaty and sticky, so before sporting their fine evening dresses, the ladies washed their undergarments in the bathtub and hung them on a curtain rod to dry.

The ghosts of schoolchildren haunt the fourth floor of Phoenix's old San Carlos Hotel.

After a joyous night of dining and dancing, the three elderly belles returned to their room in high spirits. But one look in the bathroom and their joy turned to rage. Someone had tied knots in all their underwear!

Angry at such an invasion of privacy, the women lost no time in questioning the bellboys and the cleaning staff, who each insisted, "I didn't do it!" Unable to find the culprit, the ladies checked out in a huff.

Who would do such a dirty deed? Although they hadn't told the women, the entire staff knew who would. Leone Jensen was up to her ghostly tricks again. Leone had been pulling pranks on the seventh floor since May 7, 1928, when the twenty-two-year-old threw herself off the seventh-floor roof. It was Saturday night, and Leone, who was a guest at the hotel, was waiting in an elegant white gown for her date to sweep her off to a local dance. But her love, who was a

A ghostly woman in white haunts the seventh-floor hallway, guest rooms, and sometimes even the bathrooms.

bellboy at a nearby hotel, never arrived. Brokenhearted, Leone climbed to the roof and took her life. Today, her white form is seen floating down the hall, leaning over sleeping guests, or rearranging the wash.

On the floors below, Leone has neighbors. Three little boys have been laughing and running through the halls for sixty-eight years. No one knows who they are, but they love to wake up guests in the middle of the night. When angry adults peer into the halls to catch them at their games, nobody's there! The hotel was built in 1927 where an old school stood, but no one knows why the boys remained. Revenge for bad teachers? And what about Leone? Is she jealous of women who go out dancing? Perhaps you can check in and check it out.

The white figure seen on the seventh floor is believed to be the ghost of a broken-hearted young woman who jumped off the roof.

Bird Cage Theatre, Tombstone

HAUNTED BY
A cast of Wild Westerners

The Bird Cage Theatre was the wildest place in one of the wildest towns of the Old West. For twenty-four hours a day, the dance hall saloon entertained the likes of Deputy Marshall Wyatt Earp, Doc Holliday, and the Clanton gang, who later shot it out with Earp at the OK Corral.

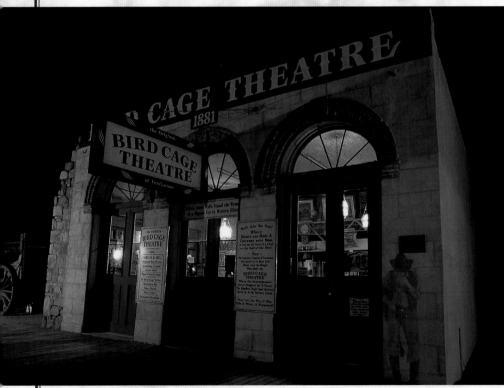

Tombstone's most haunted place is the Bird Cage Theatre, where numerous phantom gunslingers keep the old saloon hopping.

The Bird Cage was boarded up in 1885, but the partying didn't stop. Old-timers reported ghostly piano playing and singing coming from the empty hall. When it re-opened in 1934 as a tourist site, the phantoms of the Old West kicked up their heels again.

Lucky visitors hear the songs of saloon

girls, smell cigar smoke, and sometimes see a man with a clipboard float across the stage. Hanging from the ceiling are small booths called cribs, where Wild Westerners visited their favorite girls. It was in one of these cribs that the owners angered a few dead gunfighters.

Bill Hunley, Jr., was a little boy when his father decided to put wooden statues of old gunslingers in the cribs. One was Wyatt Earp. He was dressed in a fancy black suit and hat, and was put in the best crib in the house. When little Bill and his sister ran into the theater the next morning, Earp's hat had fallen off his head onto a poker table twelve feet below. They put it back and left. The next morning, and every morning after, the hat was back on the same table, no matter how many times little Bill returned it to Earp. Did Wyatt hate his hat? No one knew, until a visiting historian told the Hunleys that they had put Earp in the Clantons' favorite crib. His mortal enemies wanted him out! They moved Earp to the next crib, and his hat stayed put.

Psychics claim there may be as many as seventeen ghosts living it up in the Bird Cage. It could be the longest-running ghost party in history.

Even the statue of Tombstone's most famous gunman, Wyatt Earp, far left, draws challenges from dead outlaws.

New Mexico

Double Eagle Restaurant, Mesilla

HAUNTED BY

Armando and Inez

Have you ever been scared to death your parents wouldn't like your boyfriend or girlfriend? Back in the 1850s, a young man named Armando was, and for good reason!

Armando and Inez give unsuspecting diners a ghostly greeting in the Carlotta Room.

In the 1800s, the Double Eagle Restaurant was Armando's home.

Armando lived in a big house on the central plaza of Mesilla, then a small Mexican town in southern Arizona, near Las Cruces. His family was very rich and noble, and wanted only the best for Armando. They introduced him to the prettiest, most proper girls in town. But Armando wasn't interested. His heart secretly belonged to a maid in his own house named Inez. But he could tell no one, especially not his mother.

However, Armando's mother was suspicious, and one day she saw her son disappear into Inez's room. Blind with rage, she grabbed a pair of scissors and burst into the room. She stabbed over and over at the bed, but to her horror, she killed Armando along with Inez. Today the young lovers live out their tragic romance in the Double Eagle Restaurant, Armando's old home. At night, the restaurant is armed with motion detectors, which sense any human movement. Even though the alarms never ring, when the staff opens in the morning, they find chairs tipped over and broken glasses scattered on the floor. Guests who eat in the Carlotta Room, the lovers' old bedroom, see Inez's transparent face peeking around the corner, sitting in an old velvet chair, or reflected in the room's mirrors.

Armando is more showy. He enters the Carlotta Room as a cold breeze, sometimes sweeping entire place settings from the table. Once, eighty crystal glasses flew off a shelf in front of a room full of terrified onlookers! It is said that Armando doesn't like crystal. No one knows why.

If you decide to visit the restaurant, and eat in the Carlotta Room, be sure to take a picture. Every now and then, Inez pops up in family photos taken around the table, and you can see right through her! Maybe she'll show up in yours.

The Lodge at Cloudcroft

HAUNTED BY
Rebecca

There was a time when the beautiful Rebecca was the apple of every eye at the elegant Lodge at Cloudcroft. Until one night in 1915, when her lumberjack boyfriend arrived and found her in the arms of another man. Shortly after, the redhaired maid mysteriously disappeared forever. Or did she?

Eighty years later, a lodge guest prepared his morning bath and came downstairs for a newspaper. Upon his return, he discovered an unknown woman splashing in his tub.

"Excuse me, miss, but I think you've got the wrong room," he said. "This is *my* bath."

The woman just smiled and ignored him. Flustered and angry, the man stormed down to the front desk.

"I asked for a private bath, not a shared bath," the man complained. "There's a redhaired woman in my tub right now!"

"We don't know of any redheaded guest," the clerk at the front desk told him, but the man persisted. He decided to wait in the lobby and catch her when she checked out.

Rebecca's portrait hangs in the lodge's bar, where she plays most of her tricks.

25

Well, she never did check out, and most likely the ghost of Rebecca never will. She's having too much fun. The restaurant is named after her, where she's been seen dancing late at night and playing the piano. In the Red Dog Saloon, Rebecca's haunting portrait oversees her mischief—glasses of red wine sometimes explode on couples' tables or ashtrays move on their own.

Her practical jokes seem to happen anywhere in the Lodge, but her favorite room is 101, the Governor's Suite. Guests receive mysterious phone calls in the middle of the night, and when the room is empty, the hotel switchboard lights up with calls coming from the room! Rebecca is treated like a celebrity by the hotel staff; everyone seems to delight in her hoaxes. Look closely at her portrait, and maybe you too can spot that wily redhead up to her old tricks.

The first face to greet guests is Rebecca's, whose foyer mask eyes all who enter.

The Lodge at Cloudcroft is haunted by a beautiful maid who mysteriously disappeared eighty years ago.

Old Santa Fe Trail Books & Coffeehouse

A teenage girl

Close to Halloween a few years ago, Tonia Gould was training her new bookstore employees, who were gathered in the children's book room. Just as she began to speak, the books on the top of each shelf began flying across the room

The teenage ghost in the bookstore tries to make friends in the strangest ways.

and onto the floor, as if someone was running down the row knocking them off with a hand.

The new workers were stunned, but Tonia just laughed. "Maybe I'd better tell you about our ghost first," she said.

When Tonia bought this 1903 house and turned it into a book and food store, it came with a lonely ghost who was searching for a playmate.

The tricks started in the kitchen. Alone, early in the morning, the baker noticed objects disappearing. First her eyeglasses would vanish from her apron pocket and later reappear under a pot or on a shelf. Next, she would feel a presence behind her, and an invisible hand would untie her apron strings. As the spooky pranks continued, Tonia wondered if she might have a ghost joker on her hands. But who?

One morning, Tonia was talking to an employee working behind the bar. They faced a big mirror that showed the room

The bookstore sits on the Old Santa Fe Trail and may be haunted by a dead pioneer.

behind. Suddenly, they both stopped talking and stared into the mirror. Reflected there was a small Mexican girl, about fourteen years old. She had long brown hair and wore a fancy white party dress. When they turned around to look at her, she was gone!

Tonia had finally met her friendly ghost, but where did she come from? No one had died in the old house, so Tonia believed the girl must have been an early pioneer who had given up her ghost on the Santa Fe Trail, where the bookstore stands today.

Tonia's favorite ghostly joke happened one September night. A customer was

searching for a particular book. Tonia knew she had a copy; she had seen it the day before. But they looked and looked, and couldn't find it. Just as they were ready to give up, a book fell from the top of a shelf into the customer's hands. It was the book he had asked for!

Tonia feels protected by her silly ghost and believes she's just looking for a friend to share in her mischief. When Tonia is in her office late at night, and her door suddenly opens and closes, opens and closes, she says. "I know you're there, but I can't play right now." Her door closes softly, and the house goes quiet. But only for that moment.

*Bookstore staff have seen volumes fly off shelves onto the floor—
and sometimes even into the hands of amazed customers.*

St. James Hotel, Cimarron

HAUNTED BY

T. J. Wright, Mary Lambert, and Woody the Imp

There's a wicked ghost locked up in Room 18 of the St. James Hotel. You won't see a number over the room, and you certainly can't rent the room, even if you could find it. When past owners tried to remodel the room, they were attacked by a swirling ball of energy or they found their new furnishings thrown against a wall. When Perry Champion first bought the St. James four years ago, stories about Room 18 prompted him to lock the door permanently, to let this nasty spook rest in peace.

The hotel owner keeps a nasty ghost locked up behind this door. Room 18 is never rented out.

In this spooky second-floor room guests often smell the mysterious perfume of Mary Lambert, the wife of the first owner.

But Perry was mystified. There were other ghosts in the hotel, but no mean ones. Mary Lambert, the wife of the first owner, haunts Room 17. When she's nearby, the air fills with the thick, sweet smell of roses—Mary's favorite perfume. The fragrance moves around the room and into other parts of the hotel. Sometimes guests in Mary's old room will unpack, go downstairs, and return to find their bags packed and by the door! That's as mean as Mary gets.

In the dining room there's a tricky little ghost named Woody the Imp. A few people have seen a midget man darting around the tables, but mainly the invisible imp likes to explode glasses, hide objects from waitresses, and blow out and relight candles.

So Perry wanted to know how the phantom in 18 got so mean. He invited a psychic to investigate. After an hour in the room the psychic said that the ghost of a gambler was living in the room. One night in the 1880s, he won the hotel in a poker game, and when he came back the next day to claim ownership, he was shot in the back. His name is T. J., and he thinks he owns the place.

Perry looked through the old 1800s register. Legends like Jesse James, Wyatt Earp, Buffalo Bill Cody, and Annie Oakley were all guests. In the year 1881, he found the name T. J. Wright—with no checkout date.

Perry couldn't believe it. He had a ghost for a business partner. So Perry grabbed a bottle of whiskey and two glasses and went to Room 18. He sat down, poured two drinks, and welcomed T. J. as his partner. Perry finished his drink and left. The next day he checked the room. T. J.'s whiskey glass was empty, and the room, which had always been cold, was warm!

A night in the historic St. James is truly an otherworldly experience. From the bullet holes in the restaurant ceiling to the pictures of outlaws and lawmen on the walls, the St. James is where history comes alive, in more ways than one.

A cast of Wild West phantoms spook the St. James Hotel, where gambling and gunfights brought many cowboys to unnatural ends.

OKLAHOMA

Stone Lion Inn, Guthrie

HAUNTED BY

Augusta

Are you brave enough to spend the night in a funeral home turned hotel? If you stay at the spooky Stone Lion Inn, there's a chance this former dead house might come alive to haunt you. But not in the way you imagine!

Although this house changed from a funeral home to a fancy inn, some of the former residents may have stayed on.

Becky Luker wasn't scared when she bought the eerie mansion in 1986 for her dream inn. But from the very first night, when she and her two sons, Ral and Grant, moved in on the third floor, the nights came alive with mysterious sounds. Between 10 P.M. and midnight, as they listened in the dark, a second-floor door would open and close, followed by the sound of tiny feet climbing the back staircase to their bedroom.

Now Becky was scared, so scared she called the police. Their repeated searches found nothing, but the sounds continued. Gradually, the ghostly footsteps came closer and closer, until one night the Lukers watched in amazement as an unseen hand opened and closed the four closet doors in their bedroom. From inside the closets came quiet, eerie laughter.

Little Ral kept his toys neatly arranged in one of the closets. But to his surprise, when he opened it the next morning, his toys were strewn all over the floor.

Was this mysterious midnight visitor a former resident of the old funeral home? Becky didn't know until one day when Ral left his toy closet and ran to the kitchen in a rage. "Mom," he said, "that little girl is playing with my toys again." Becky was astonished; her son had seen the ghost! But who was this little girl ghost?

Soon after, an old woman who once lived in the mansion told Becky a story, and the mystery was solved. Eighty years ago, a family with three children lived there. They too kept their toys in the third-floor closets. At 10 P.M. each

Ghostly footsteps are heard on this back stairway, which leads to the third floor.

At night, in a second-floor guest room, a caring spirit covers these dolls with a blanket.

night, as their parents slept, the kids would sneak upstairs to the closets and play until midnight.

One of the children was little Augusta. When she was eight, she caught a bad cough, and a nurse was called to the house. By mistake, the nurse gave Augusta too much medicine, and she died that night in her bed. When Ral heard Augusta's sad story, he bought puzzles and dolls for the girl ghost, to keep her happy forever.

Today, guests at the inn still hear Augusta's ghostly footsteps on the back stairs, and sometimes the gentle spirit will stroke a sleeping guest's hair or face. And should Augusta's dolls be left uncovered in their crib now on the second floor, a blanket will mysteriously cover them at night to keep them warm.

Fort Washita, near Madill

Jane
the headless ghost

In 1843, Fort Washita was built to protect the local Chickasaw Indians from white men seeking revenge for past Indian raids. But the soldiers couldn't protect poor Jane, who lived at the fort as an officer's wife.

Riding her horse back from town one day, Jane was ambushed by robbers and killed. To hide her identity, the bandits cut off her head and threw it into the Red River. Indian legend says that a body without a head cannot see its way to the spirit world, and locals claim a headless horsewoman rides the rivers and woods looking for her lost body part.

But when Jane wasn't looking for her head, she was causing others to lose theirs. Families staying in the old officers' building told of frightening encounters with a big, yellow-eyed black cat who said nasty things as she chased them. Other times, Jane has appeared as a glowing white form in the kitchen. She has tried to lure her speechless victims from the house with mysterious promises of wealth, her words coming from a headless body.

Soon, word of the headless haunter spread, and no one dared live at the closed fort. The officers' building fell apart, and Jane was left with broken stone walls and creeping vines to spook.

In 1962, Fort Washita became a state park, and the building next to Jane's was restored. Perhaps she's jealous, because she tricks the staff by unlocking and locking doors, and turning the lights off and on. But Jane mainly hovers in the rock ruins, and nighttime ghost-hunting parties hope to sneak a peek at the head-less ghost or the terrible talking cat.

Jane, the headless horsewoman, still haunts the ruins of her old home at Fort Washita.

TEXAS

Catfish Plantation Restaurant, Waxahachie

HAUNTED BY

Elizabeth, Caroline, and Will

The sign at the entrance of the Catfish Plantation Restaurant says, "If

The Catfish Plantation Restaurant and an actual phantom, photographed by a restaurant customer as it hovered over his table.

you have a ghostly experience, please tell us!" This old house turned Cajun eatery may have a spicy menu, but it's the off-menu ghosts that add the real fire to dining out. The Catfish Plantation Restaurant may be the most haunted place in Texas, and unlike most hauntings, the ghosts here aren't shy.

So many strange things happen here that the owners have three notebooks full of letters written by guests who were served more than they ordered. Silverware moves, objects drop onto tables from thin air, writing appears on windows, broken clocks start to chime, the radio changes stations automatically. Diners who ask for a ghostly sign are often touched on the arm or face. One little girl who asked to meet a ghost was on her way to the bathroom when she was passed by a white blurry ball. It touched her face, flew to the dining room, and disappeared.

Psychics say that the Catfish Plantation is a powerful portal to the spirit world, like a revolving door that whisks ghosts and objects from their world to ours. That's why odd things materialize on guests' tables.

Three main ghosts share the restaurant: Elizabeth, Caroline, and Will. Elizabeth lived in the house in the 1920s and was strangled on her wedding day by a jealous lover. She is a kindly spirit and is responsible for the touches guests feel and for the moving cold spots. Some people see her in the front window dressed in white. Others are followed home by this curious ghost.

Caroline grew old in the house and died of a stroke in 1970. She is a thrower and a slammer. While alive, Caroline loved to cook for her family, and now, when she is fed up with all the strangers in her house, she throws coffee cups and plates, and slams doors. She hates alcohol and constantly breaks the wine glasses stacked in the kitchen.

Will was an old farmer who lived in the house right after Elizabeth did. He's a peaceful spirit and doesn't do much except hang out on the porch. Police officers driving by at night have seen a man in overalls standing there, but as they approach he disappears.

This is a wonderful place to have a gentle ghost encounter at any time of day, with others around. Go, ask for a sign, tell Elizabeth you'd like to meet her, and maybe you'll be making an eerie entry in the ghost book out front.

Driskill Hotel, Austin

HAUNTED BY

The Old Caretaker, Peter J. Lawless

Deshay Bunton has seen a lot in his twelve years working at the Driskill, Austin's elegant hotel from the Wild West days. But late one night, while cleaning the carpets on the fifth floor, he saw too much.

The Driskill had always given Deshay goose bumps because of the stories about the fourth floor, where several suicides and murders had trapped unlucky souls in their rooms. But Deshay was on the fifth floor that night, and even though he was all alone, he wasn't thinking about ghosts.

It was after midnight as Deshay pushed his vacuum

The Driskill is Austin's oldest, and most haunted, hotel.

down the hall and past the elevators. Suddenly, out of nowhere, an ice-cold wind poured over him from behind. The hair on the back of his neck tingled with fear. Time to get out of here, Deshay said to himself. Quickly, he shut off the vacuum and turned to get on the elevator.

Seated on the couch next to the elevator was a man. "Good evening," Deshay said as he pushed the down button. When the man didn't answer, Deshay turned

around and took a good look at him. The man wore old-style Western clothes and had his legs crossed. But the man Deshay stared at wasn't all there; he could see right through him! Just then, the elevator arrived, and Deshay leaped into it.

Deshay didn't tell anyone about his ghostly encounter. It might sound crazy, he thought. But he and other staff members started hearing stories from guests on the fifth floor who had heard chains rattling in the hall and a few in Room 537

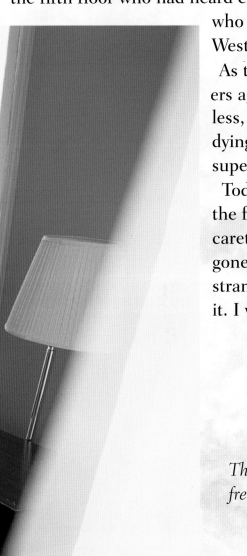

who had woken up to see a transparent man dressed in Western clothes, sitting, reading a newspaper.

As the stories were pieced together, all the hotel workers agreed. It must be the old caretaker, Peter J. Lawless, who had lived in Room 537 for thirty years, dying there in 1920. He was still watching the hotel, supervising the upkeep.

Today, Deshay is the maintenance chief, and when the fifth-floor lights flicker late at night, he knows the caretaker is watching. The couch by the elevator is gone—too many complaints from guests feeling strange, uncomfortable sensations when they sat on it. I wonder why?

The ghost of Peter J. Lawless, the old caretaker, is frequently seen in his old room.

Fort Concho, San Angelo

HAUNTED BY
Dead soldiers

O ld forts seem to attract ghosts like a picnic draws ants. Built right after the Civil War, Fort Concho is no exception. Unlike the headless horror of Oklahoma's Fort Washita (page 38), Fort Concho's ghosts appear to be soldiers who won't give up the fight.

Spirit troops have been seen all over the restored outpost but mainly in the old barracks building where they once lived. Conrad McClure is a tour guide in the

Fort employees have seen a ghost soldier inside the barracks where he once lived.

barracks, and in his fifteen years there, he has seen more strange things than anyone else.

One December day, Conrad prepared for the fort's Christmas celebration, stoking the wood fire in the cold barracks. As he watched the fire, a sudden movement caught his eye. A shadowy figure brushed by him, and Conrad could see the outline of his military hat and dress. Just as quickly, the apparition disappeared.

Conrad wasn't scared. On other occasions, he had heard footsteps in the barracks and the clip-clop sounds of military boots on the porch outside. But he was curious who this soldier might be. Looking through the fort's old records, Conrad read the account of Second Sergeant Cunningham. It seems the sergeant had a passion for spirits, the alcohol kind, and was hospitalized with liver disease.

Several of Fort Concho's buildings, including the old headquarters, have ghosts from its frontier days.

He was released for the holidays, but he died in the barracks on Christmas Day, 1883. He was the only one on record to die in the building.

Conrad believes Sergeant Cunningham as well as the other ghosts are guarding the fort and are not there to scare people. He's seen the shadow of the dead army surgeon near the old hospital, lights turning off and on in the empty Headquarters Building, and oil lamps swinging on their own in the barracks. Once, he was locked out of Officers Building 9, and he had the only key! It's in this building that others have reported hearing a ghostly argument between an officer and his wife.

Although the Western frontier may have disappeared years ago, the spirit frontier is alive and well at Fort Concho. Walk or drive through at night, and look for the phantoms still on duty.

Many San Angelo residents won't come to the fort after dark fearing the "night life" on the grounds.